SUDOKU QUILTS

Cyndi Hershey

Martingale®
& COMPANY

Credits

President • Nancy J. Martin

CEO • Daniel J. Martin

COO • Tom Wierzbicki

Publisher • Jane Hamada

Editorial Director • Mary V. Green

Managing Editor • Tina Cook

Technical Editor • Ellen Pahl

Copy Editor • Sheila Chapman Ryan

Design Director • Stan Green

Illustrators • Wendy Slotboom and Laurel Strand

Cover and Text Designer • Shelly Garrison

Photographer • Brent Kane

Sudoku Quilts
© 2007 by Cyndi Hershey

That Patchwork Place® is an imprint of Martingale & Company®.

Martingale & Company
20205 144th Ave. NE
Woodinville, WA 98072-8478 USA
www.martingale-pub.com

Printed in China
12 11 10 09 08 07   8 7 6 5 4 3 2 1

Library of Congress Cataloging-in-Publication Data
Library of Congress Control Number: 2006026553

ISBN: 978-1-56477-731-7

Mission Statement

Dedicated to providing quality products
and service to inspire creativity.

Dedication

To my parents, who provided a home filled with creativity. You made sure that I learned to love and appreciate all forms of art and music, thus enabling me to always see the possibilities.

Acknowledgments

Heartfelt thanks to:

- Jim, Christopher, and Amanda for putting up with all of my creative endeavors over the years. Love you lots.

- Mary Green and Karen Soltys for encouraging me to keep trying. Your friendship and support have meant a great deal to me.

- The New Hampshire Pines—Doris Adomsky, Sally Malley, Carol Mirynowski, and Janet Schneider— for your help with binding quilts and your ongoing friendship. We are kindred spirits!

- Everyone at Country Quiltworks for your suggestions, support, and most of all, your skill at unsewing! You're the best.

- Mary Covey and Kim Pope—your machine quilting is exquisite and helped my quilts to look their very best.

- My friends at P&B Textiles, who are always ready to help and encourage me. Boundless thanks.

Contents

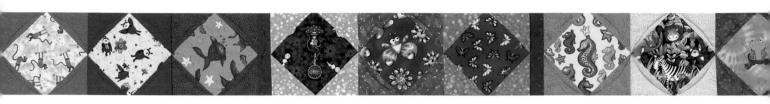

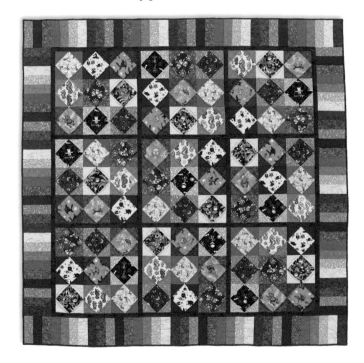

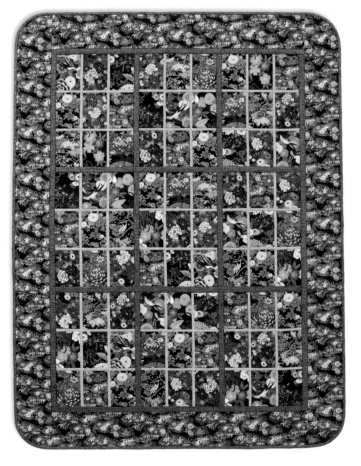

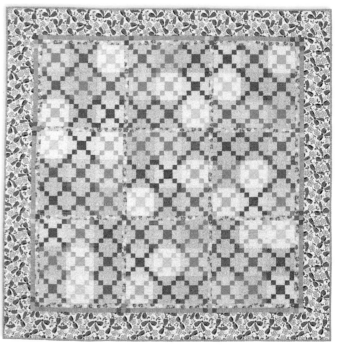

Sudoku is a placement puzzle that uses numbers. Most people assume that this puzzle is from Japan or another Asian country. Not true! In fact, this puzzle has its origins in the United Kingdom, where it has been played for many years under several different names. The Japanese caught on to this puzzle game and gave it the name Sudoku—*su* meaning "number" and *doku* meaning "single." Number games are much more popular in Japan than word games, and this game reached a frenzied craze in the early 2000s. It gained popularity in the United States a few years ago and now you can find books full of Sudoku puzzles. You can also find a puzzle in most Sunday newspapers and even in the airline magazines that are in the seat pockets of most airplanes!

So, how does it work? The puzzle grid is made up of nine large squares that are each divided into nine smaller squares. The numbers 1 through 9 are placed only one time within each smaller square. Additionally, a number may appear only *once* in each vertical or horizontal row. There are usually a few numbers already filled in on the grid to get you started. The more numbers that are initially provided, the easier the puzzle will be. Here is an example of how you may see a puzzle presented and the subsequent completed puzzle.

9	4	5	2	8	7	6	3	1
3	8	7	9	1	6	5	2	4
2	1	6	5	3	4	8	7	9
8	2	9	1	5	3	7	4	6
7	3	1	4	6	9	2	8	5
5	6	4	8	7	2	9	1	3
1	9	2	7	4	5	3	6	8
6	7	8	3	9	1	4	5	2
4	5	3	6	2	8	1	9	7

Blue numbers are part of the original puzzle.
Red numbers are filled in to complete the puzzle.

How do you solve it? Through logic. It's that simple—and that difficult. You will find that with practice you are able to establish methods that work well for you. You just need to get a pencil (and eraser) and jump in!

Sudoku Quilts

Shortly after I started working with these number puzzles, I realized that the puzzle grid is just like the Double Nine Patch block used in quilting. I wondered what would happen if the numbers were replaced with nine different sets of blocks—one set for each number. The more I played with the concept, the more possibilities became apparent to me.

Blocks. Block sets can be based on nine different color families, nine different-style blocks, nine different block centers, or nine different fabric motifs, to name a few examples. The possibilities for creativity are endless! You can certainly use any type of block that you desire, but I suggest blocks with simple construction because they are small and you need 81 of them! Of course, you can make larger blocks if you want a larger quilt.

Sashing. Each of the four patterns in this book has a different sashing treatment. The nine large squares are separated from each other with obvious sashing. If you like a more subtle look, you can substitute a folded flange or unfilled piping instead of true sashing to give just a hint of separation between the blocks. If the small blocks relate well to each other or continue a pattern, then there is no need for sashing between them. However, if the small blocks blend together or become visually confusing, sashing can separate and add definition to the small blocks as well.

Borders. Border options are unlimited. As you create your own designs, feel free to experiment with the borders.

Have fun creating your own Sudoku quilt. Select a block, borrow a sashing idea from one quilt, and use a border idea from another!

Making the Blocks

To keep the flavor of a Sudoku puzzle, each quilt pattern includes a "puzzle solution." To use these solutions, assign a number—1 through 9—to each set of identical blocks. Then, lay out your blocks following the numbers in the puzzle solution. Once you have all the blocks in position, it helps to label the blocks before you pick them up to sew. I used the following code for my blocks: 1, 2, and 3 for the horizontal rows and A, B, and C for the blocks in each vertical column.

	A	B	C
Row 1	1A	1B	1C
Row 2	2A	2B	2C
Row 3	3A	3B	3C

I suggest that you make paper labels that read 1A, 1B, 1C; 2A, 2B, 2C; and 3A, 3B, 3C. Pin a label to each small block. Slide all the blocks onto a cutting mat and carry them to the sewing machine. When the large block is finished, lay it back down in place and use the paper labels for the next set of small blocks. Once all the large blocks are complete, use the labels again to help keep those in order as well.

Press both your small and large blocks well; they will have many seams. Press all seams after they are sewn in the direction of the arrows in the illustrations.

HELPFUL HINT: Spray sizing (found in discount or grocery stores) is very helpful when pressing to keep the blocks as flat as possible during the construction process.

Sudoku Swaps

Sudoku quilts are ideal to make with your quilting friends! Gather eight of your quilting friends together (you're the ninth) and provide a set of block instructions. Be specific about the type and color of fabrics that each person should use. Be sure each quilter understands that she is to make 81 identical blocks. When finished, exchange the blocks so that everyone has one set (nine blocks) of each type. Give a different Sudoku puzzle solution to each person. Each quilter then completes the quilt using her own sashing and border ideas. When the quilts are finished, it will be amazing to see how different the quilts are!

Basic Quiltmaking

The projects in this book use basic cutting and piecing techniques that are familiar to most quilters. If you would like detailed instructions for rotary cutting and machine piecing, I recommend *The Quilter's Quick Reference Guide* by Candace Eisner Strick (Martingale & Company, 2004). In this comprehensive book you will also find complete instructions for finishing quilts, including cutting and sewing borders, preparing quilt backings, basic quilting techniques, and sewing both straight-grain and bias binding.

Designed and sewn by Cyndi Hershey. Quilted by Kim Pope.

Finished quilt: 70½" x 70½"

Finished small block: 6" x 6"

Finished large block: 18" x 18"

BITS AND PIECES: This quilt is made using a Square-in-a-Square block. Conversation prints make a cheerful quilt for a child, but you could easily substitute nine different floral or vintage prints for the center squares to create a completely different look. Even better—try using nine different photos printed on fabric for the center squares to make a unique memory quilt!

Materials

Yardage is based on 42"-wide fabric.

- ½ yard *each* of 9 different conversation prints for center squares of small blocks*
- ½ yard *each* of 9 different tonal prints for corners of small blocks and pieced border
- 1¼ yards of blue fabric for sashing, inner border, and binding
- 4½ yards of fabric for backing
- 75" x 75" piece of batting
- 4¾" square of see-through template plastic for fussy cutting (optional)
- Featherweight nonwoven fusible interfacing for fussy cutting (optional)

Yardage allows for fussy cutting the center squares of the blocks. If you choose not to fussy cut the squares, you will need only ⅓ yard of each fabric.

Cutting

From *each* of the 9 conversation prints, cut:
9 squares, 4¾" x 4¾" (81 total)*

From *each* of the 9 tonal prints, cut:
2 strips, 3⅞" x 42"; crosscut into 18 squares, 3⅞" x 3⅞". Cut each square in half diagonally to yield 36 triangles (324 total).
3 strips, 2½" x 42" (27 total)

From the blue fabric, cut:
12 strips, 1½" x 42"; crosscut 3 of the strips into 6 rectangles, 1½" x 18½"
8 strips, 2½" x 42"

*If fussy cutting, use the plastic template. If not fussy cutting, cut the 9 squares from 2 strips, 4¾" x 42".

Fussy-Cutting Tips

When fussy cutting, you can select a particular area of the fabric to showcase in each center square. Place the square plastic template on the right side of the fabric and center the chosen motif within the square. Trace around the template and cut out the square. Since you may be cutting off grain, here's a tip to avoid potential stretching of the fabric. *Before* tracing any squares onto the fabric, iron featherweight nonwoven fusible interfacing to the wrong side of the fabric. The fabric will now be completely stable, allowing you to cut squares at any angle. The fusible interfacing will remain in the quilt; it doesn't add any stiffness—only stability.

Making the Blocks

Pair up the center-square fabrics with the triangle fabrics. You will make nine identical blocks from each set of fabrics.

1. Sew tonal print 3⅞" triangles to opposite sides of a center square. Press. Repeat for the remaining sides of the square; press. Make nine blocks.

Make 9.

2. Repeat step 1 with the remaining sets of block fabrics to make a total of 81 blocks.

3. Assign a number, 1 through 9, to each set of blocks. Use the puzzle solution to lay out the small blocks into nine large blocks.

4	5	7	2	9	3	1	8	6
1	9	8	5	6	4	7	3	2
6	2	3	7	8	1	5	4	9
2	4	9	6	1	5	8	7	3
3	8	1	9	2	7	6	5	4
7	6	5	4	3	8	9	2	1
9	3	6	8	7	2	4	1	5
5	7	2	1	4	6	3	9	8
8	1	4	3	5	9	2	6	7

Puzzle solution

4. To make a large block, sew the small blocks together into rows. Press. Sew the rows together and press. Make nine large blocks.

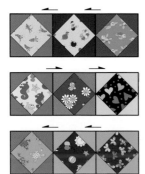 

Make 9.

Assembling the Quilt Top

1. Sew the nine blue 1½" x 42" strips together end to end. Press the seams open. From this pieced strip, cut four strips, 1½" x 56½", and two strips, 1½" x 58½".

2. Sew a blue 1½" x 18½" rectangle between each of the large blocks in the three rows. Press.

Pin for Perfection

To keep the corners and points of the small blocks aligned across the sashing, you may find it helpful to first sew one side of a sashing strip to a large block. Then, place positioning pins along the unsewn side of the sashing opposite the block corners and points. Pin the next block in place carefully, matching the corners and points to the positioning pins, and sew.

3. Sew a blue 1½" x 56½" strip between each row and press. Sew the remaining blue 1½" x 56½" strips to opposite sides of the quilt.

4. Sew a 1½" x 58½" strip to the top and bottom of the quilt. Press.

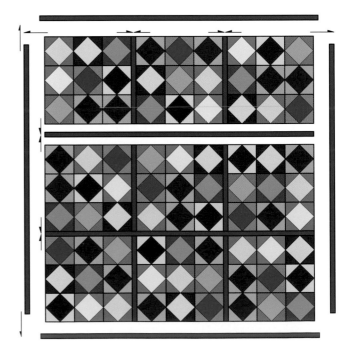

Adding the Pieced Borders

1. Sew one 2½" x 42" strip of each tonal print together on the long sides to make a strip set. Press the seams in one direction. Repeat to make three strip sets. Cut the strip sets into 15 segments, 6½" wide.

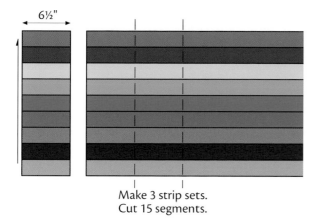

Make 3 strip sets.
Cut 15 segments.

2. To make the side borders, sew three segments together end to end, being careful to continue the pattern of fabric-color placement. Press. Make two. Remove two rectangles from one end of a remaining segment and sew them to one of the side borders, continuing the pattern of fabric placement as shown. Remove two rectangles from the opposite end of the same segment and sew them to the other side border, again matching the fabric placement. Press.

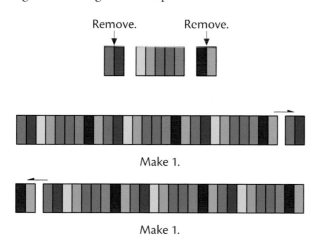

Remove.   Remove.

Make 1.

Make 1.

3. Sew the borders to opposite sides of the quilt. Press.

4. To make the top and bottom borders, repeat step 2 using four strip-set segments for each border. You will need to remove one rectangle from one end of each border. *Before* you do this, lay the borders against the quilt along the top and bottom edges to see how the colors of the rectangles work together. Reposition the borders until you find the best placement. Then, remove the extra rectangle from one end of each border. Sew the borders to the quilt and press.

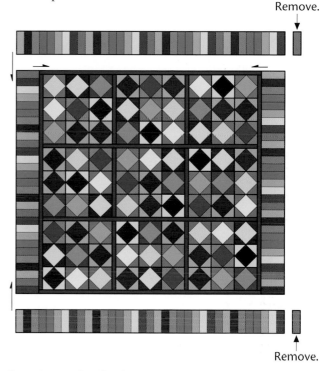

Remove.

Remove.

Finishing the Quilt

1. Layer your quilt with batting and a pieced backing; baste. Quilt as desired. If you used the fusible interfacing and want to hand quilt, use a thin, lightweight batting. The quilt shown was machine quilted with curves around each center square, providing a nice balance to the sharp angles in the quilt.

2. Trim the edges of the quilt even with the top and use the blue 2½" x 42" strips to bind the quilt.

Sudoku Windows

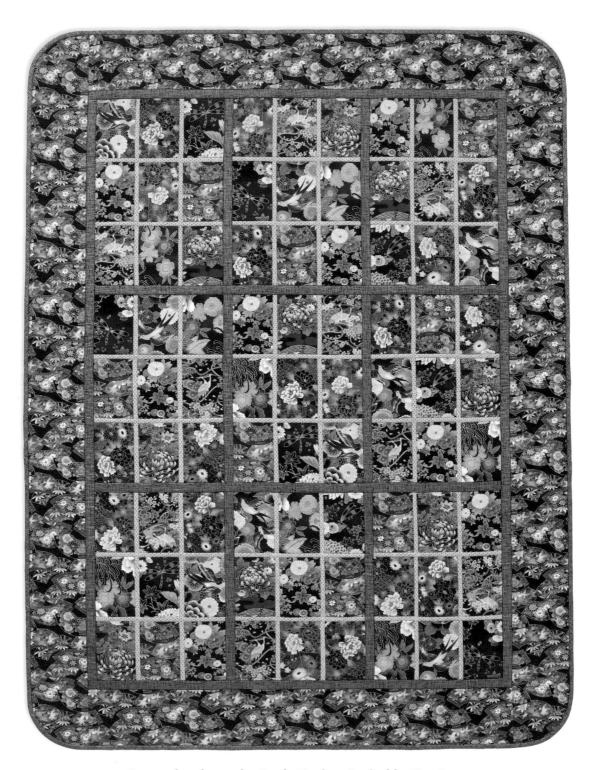

Designed and sewn by Cyndi Hershey. Quilted by Kim Pope.

Finished quilt: 55½" x 73½"
Finished small block: 4" x 6"
Finished large block: 13" x 19"

BITS AND PIECES: Sometimes less is more, and this quilt is a perfect way to use those lovely Asian prints that are available in quilt shops. But feel free to be creative—this quilt design would lend itself to using large-scale prints of any theme.

Materials

Yardage is based on 42"-wide fabric.

- 1 yard *each* of 9 different prints for small blocks*
- 2⅔ yards of red fan print for outer border**
- 1½ yards of red plaid for large-block sashing, inner border, and binding
- ½ yard of gold print for small-block sashing
- 3½ yards of fabric for backing***
- 60" x 78" piece of batting
- 4½" x 6½" piece of clear template plastic for fussy cutting (optional)
- Featherweight nonwoven fusible interfacing for fussy cutting (optional)

Yardage allows for fussy cutting the center squares of the blocks. If you choose not to fussy cut the squares, you will need only ⅓ yard of each fabric.

**Yardage for outer border is based on using a directional fabric as in the quilt shown. If you choose to use a nondirectional fabric, you will need only 2 yards.*

***Yardage allows for backing fabric to be pieced horizontally.*

Cutting

If you choose to fussy cut the blocks, refer to "Fussy-Cutting Tips" (page 9).

From *each* of the 9 different prints, cut:
9 rectangles, 4½" x 6½" (81 total)*

From the gold print, cut:
15 strips, 1" x 42"; crosscut into 54 rectangles, 1" x 6½", and 18 rectangles, 1" x 13½"

From the red plaid, cut:
12 strips, 1½" x 42"; crosscut *3* of the strips into 6 strips, 1½" x 19½"

From the remainder of the red plaid, cut:
2½"-wide bias strips to total 274"

From the red fan print, cut:
4 strips, 6½" x 42", from the crosswise grain
2 strips, 6½" x 61½", from the lengthwise grain

If you're using a nondirectional outer-border fabric, cut:
2 strips, 6½" x 55½", from the lengthwise grain
2 strips, 6½" x 61½", from the lengthwise grain

If fussy cutting, use the plastic template. If not fussy cutting, cut the 9 rectangles from 2 strips, 4½" x 42".

Making the Blocks

1. Assign a number, 1 through 9, to each set of identical rectangles that will become the small blocks. Use the puzzle solution to lay out the small blocks into nine large blocks.

3	7	1	8	6	9	5	2	4
5	8	4	1	3	2	9	6	7
6	2	9	7	4	5	1	8	3
1	3	2	5	9	6	7	4	8
4	5	6	2	7	8	3	1	9
7	9	8	4	1	3	6	5	2
8	6	7	3	2	1	4	9	5
2	1	3	9	5	4	8	7	6
9	4	5	6	8	7	2	3	1

Puzzle solution

2. Sew a gold 1" x 6½" strip between each of the small blocks in each row of the large blocks. Press. Sew a gold 1" x 13½" strip between each of the rows. Press. Make nine large blocks.

Make 9.

Assembling the Quilt Top

1. Sew a red plaid 1½" x 19½" strip between each of the large blocks as shown. Press. Make three rows.

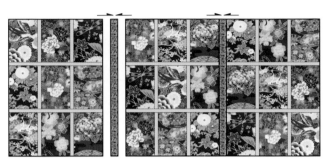

Make 3.

2. Sew the nine red plaid 1½" x 42" strips together end to end. Press the seams open. From this pieced strip, cut two strips, 1½" x 41½". Reserve the remainder of the pieced strip for the inner border. **Note:** If your fabric is wide enough, you *may* be able to use a single strip for each of the sashing strips without creating a pieced strip first.

3. Sew a 1½" x 41½" strip between each block row and sew the rows together. Press.

4. From the remainder of the red plaid strip, cut two strips, 1½" x 43½", and two strips, 1½" x 59½". Sew the 59½" strips to opposite sides of the quilt. Sew the 43½" strips to the top and bottom of the quilt. Press.

5. Sew red fan 6½" x 61½" strips to opposite sides of the quilt. Press. If your outer border is directional like the red fan print in the project quilt, continue with step 6. If your print is nondirectional, follow step 7. **Note:** The top and bottom borders were sewn on first in the quilt in the photograph. This was the most efficient use of fabric, because the strips could be cut 43½" across the grain without piecing.

6. Sew the four red fan 6½" x 42" strips together end to end, matching the print in the fabric. Press the seams open. From this pieced strip, cut two strips, 6½" x 55½".

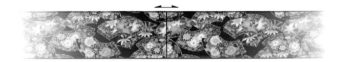

7. Sew the strips to the top and bottom of the quilt, being careful to keep the print facing in the correct direction if necessary. Press.

Finishing the Quilt

1. Layer your quilt with batting and a pieced backing; baste. Quilt as desired. The quilt shown was quilted in the ditch in all seams. The outer border contains a fan motif in the quilting.

2. Trim the edges of the quilt even with the top. Use a plate or compass to trace and cut a rounded edge at each corner, and then use the 2½"-wide bias strips to bind the quilt.

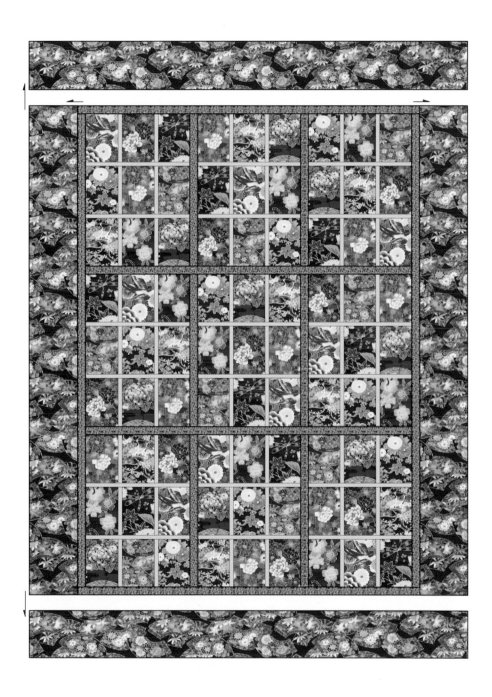

Full-Tilt Sudoku

Designed and sewn by Cyndi Hershey. Quilted by Mary Covey.

Finished quilt: 75½" x 75½"
Finished small block: 6" x 6"
Finished large block: 18" x 18"

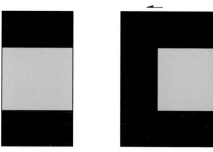

BITS AND PIECES: Simple blocks tilted back and forth give a sense of playfulness and motion to this quilt. The centers of the small blocks are tonal fabrics that showcase quilted motifs. Each set of blocks has the same quilting design throughout the quilt. For a different look, substitute an appliqué motif for the quilting design. Choose nine appliqué motifs with a common theme to give this quilt a truly original style. Any of the ideas that were suggested for "I-Spy Sudoku" (page 8) would also work well.

Materials

Yardage is based on 42"-wide fabric.

- ⅔ yard *each* of 9 different prints for small-block frames
- ⅓ yard *each* of 9 different light tonal fabrics for small-block centers
- 2⅓ yards of multicolored print for outer border
- 1⅔ yards of red tonal fabric for sashing, inner border, and binding
- ½ yard of orange tonal fabric for sashing and middle border
- 5 yards of fabric for backing
- 80" x 80" piece of batting
- 6½" square ruler or 6½" square of template plastic

Cutting

From *each* of the 9 light tonal fabrics, cut:
9 squares, 4½" x 4½" (81 total)

From *each* of the 9 prints, cut:
8 strips, 2½" x 42"; crosscut into 18 rectangles, 2½" x 4½", and 18 rectangles, 2½" x 8½" (162 total of each size)

From the red tonal fabric, cut:
12 strips, 1¼" x 42"
15 strips, 2½" x 42"

From the orange tonal fabric, cut:
13 strips, 1" x 42"

From the multicolored print, cut:
2 strips, 6½" x 63½", from the lengthwise grain
2 strips, 6½" x 75½", from the lengthwise grain
4 squares, 2½" x 2½"

Making the Blocks

Pair up each of the light center-square fabrics with the print fabrics. You will make nine identical blocks from each set of fabrics.

1. Using one set of block fabrics, sew 2½" x 4½" rectangles to opposite sides of a 4½" center square. Press. Sew 2½" x 8½" rectangles to the remaining sides of the square. Press. Repeat to make nine small blocks.

Make 9.

2. Repeat step 1 with the remaining sets of block fabrics to make a total of 81 small blocks.

3. Center the 6½" square ruler or template plastic over a small block at an angle so that the points of the square touch each edge as shown. This point is 2⁷⁄₁₆" from each corner (halfway between 2⅜" and 2½"). Trim all sides of the block. From each set of nine blocks, cut five blocks at one angle and four at the opposite angle.

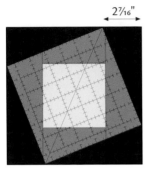
Cut 5.

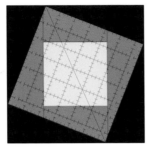
Cut 4.

4. Assign a number, 1 through 9, to each set of blocks. Use the puzzle solution to lay out the small blocks into nine large blocks. All the small blocks should slant in one direction for five of the large blocks and in the opposite direction for four of the large blocks.

8	1	3	7	6	2	9	4	5
7	4	6	3	5	9	8	2	1
2	9	5	8	4	1	7	3	6
6	3	1	4	7	8	2	5	9
4	5	7	2	9	6	1	8	3
9	8	2	5	1	3	4	6	7
3	6	4	1	2	7	5	9	8
1	2	9	6	8	5	3	7	4
5	7	8	9	3	4	6	1	2

Puzzle solution

5. Sew the small blocks together into rows and then sew the rows together to make nine large blocks. Press.

Assembling the Quilt Top

1. Sew a red 1¼" x 42" strip to both long sides of an orange 1" x 42" strip. Press. Repeat to make six strip sets. Cut 12 segments, 18½" long, for sashing.

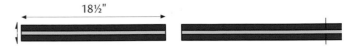
18½"

Make 6 strip sets.
Cut 2 segments per set (12 total).

2. Sew a sashing segment between the large blocks in each row. Press.

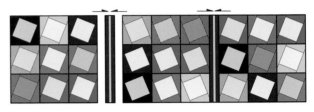
Make 3.

3. Join two multicolored 2½" squares with three sashing segments. Press. Make two for horizontal sashing.

Make 2.

4. Sew a sashing strip from step 3 between each of the block rows and sew the rows together. Press.
5. Sew seven of the red 2½" x 42" strips end to end. From this pieced strip, cut two strips, 2½" x 58½", and two strips, 2½" x 62½".
6. Sew the 58½" strips to the top and bottom of the quilt. Press. Then sew the 62½" strips to the sides of the quilt and press.
7. Sew the remaining orange 1" x 42" strips together end to end. Press seams open. From this pieced strip, cut two strips, 1" x 62½", and two strips, 1" x 63½".
8. Sew the 62½" strips to the top and bottom of the quilt, and then sew the 63½" strips to the sides of the quilt, pressing after each.

9. Sew the multicolored 6½" x 63½" strips to the top and bottom of the quilt. Press. Sew the multicolored 6½" x 75½" strips to the sides of the quilt. Press.

Finishing the Quilt

1. Layer your quilt with batting and a pieced backing; baste. Quilt as desired. Refer to the photograph at right and "Bits and Pieces" (page 17) for quilting details.

2. Trim the edges of the quilt even with the quilt top and use the remaining red 2½" x 42" strips to bind the quilt.

Using a different fabric color and quilting motif for each block makes each one unique.

Sudoku Chains

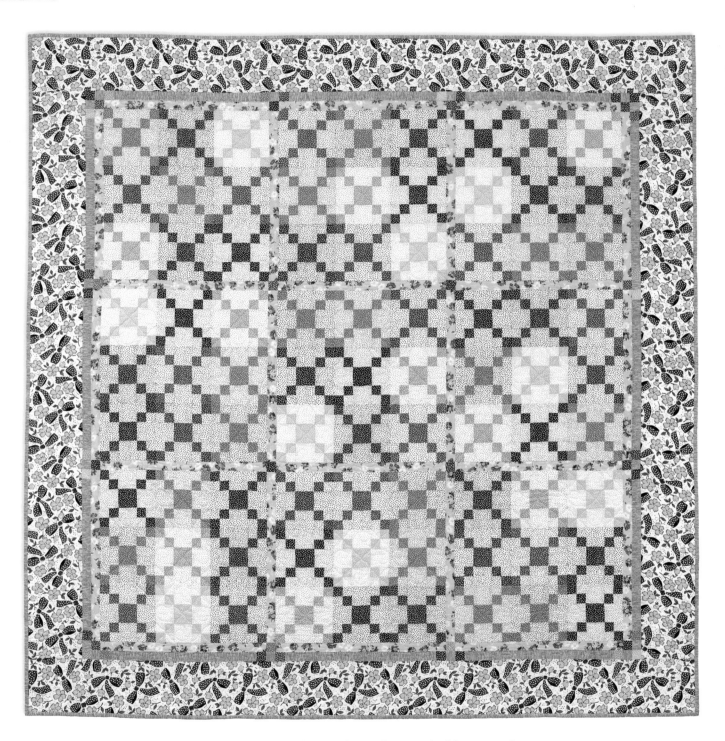

Designed and made by Cyndi Hershey. Quilted by Mary Covey.

Finished quilt: 72½" x 72½"
Finished small block: 6" x 6"
Finished large block: 18" x 18"

BITS AND PIECES: This quilt is made of blocks that look like a chain when combined; light fabrics are used for the background and darker fabrics are used for the chains. The fabrics in the quilt shown include light dot fabrics for the background that are the reverse of the dark dot fabrics for the chains. These fabrics make it appear that the chains are connecting through the large blocks. Small squares in the sashing and borders continue the diagonal pattern. A yellow, floral-print sashing adds softness to the dot fabrics. To make your quilt more graphic, increase the level of contrast within the small blocks as well as in the sashing and borders.

Materials

Yardage is based on 42"-wide fabric.

- ½ yard *each* of 9 light dot prints for small blocks
- ⅓ yard *each* of 9 dark dot prints for small blocks, sashing squares, and border squares
- 2¼ yards of purple-and-yellow print for outer border
- 1 yard of light purple print for middle border and binding
- ⅝ yard of yellow print for sashing and inner border
- 4¾ yards of fabric for backing
- 77" x 77" piece of batting

Cutting

From *each* of the 9 dark dot prints, cut:
4 strips, 1½" x 42"; crosscut one strip into a minimum of 5 squares, 1½" x 1½" (36 strips total; 44 squares total are needed of assorted colors)
1 strip, 2½" x 42"; crosscut into 9 squares, 2½" x 2½" (81 total)

From *each* of the 9 light dot prints, cut:
3 strips, 1½" x 42" (27 total)
3 strips, 2½" x 42"; crosscut into 36 squares, 2½" x 2½" (324 total)

From the yellow print, cut:
12 strips, 1½" x 42"; crosscut into 24 strips, 1½" x 18½"

From the light purple print, cut:
7 strips, 1½" x 42"; crosscut into 16 squares, 1½" x 1½", and 12 strips, 1½" x 16½"
8 strips, 2½" x 42"

From the lengthwise grain of the purple-and-yellow print, cut:
2 strips, 6½" x 60½"
2 strips, 6½" x 72½"

Making the Blocks

Pair up the dark and light dot fabrics. You will make nine identical blocks from each set of fabrics.

1. Using one set of block fabrics, sew a dark dot print 1½" x 42" strip to a light dot print 1½" x 42" strip along the long sides. Press. Make three strip sets. Cut the strip sets into 72 segments, 1½" wide.

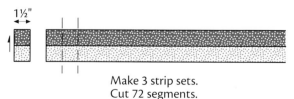

Make 3 strip sets.
Cut 72 segments.

2. Sew two 1½" segments together to make a four-patch unit. Press. Make 36.

Make 36.

3. Arrange four units from step 2 with four light dot 2½" squares and one dark dot 2½" square as shown. Sew together into rows. Press. Sew the rows together and press. Make nine blocks.

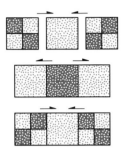 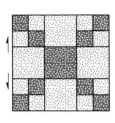

Make 9.

4. Repeat steps 1–3 for each set of block fabrics to make a total of 81 blocks.

5. Assign a number, 1 through 9, to each set of blocks. Use the puzzle solution to lay out the small blocks into nine large blocks.

2	5	6	9	7	8	1	3	4
3	7	9	2	4	1	6	8	5
4	8	1	5	3	6	9	2	7
6	1	4	7	2	3	8	5	9
5	9	2	8	1	4	7	6	3
8	3	7	6	5	9	4	1	2
1	2	8	3	9	7	5	4	6
7	4	5	1	6	2	3	9	8
9	6	3	4	8	5	2	7	1

Puzzle solution

Seams Right

For *each* large block, rotate the small blocks (maintaining position) so that seams are facing in opposite directions within rows as well as from row to row. The majority of all seams will face in opposite directions, enabling you to achieve accurate seam intersections.

6. Sew the small blocks together into rows. Press. Sew the rows together and press. Make nine large blocks.

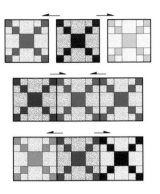 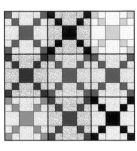

Make 9.

Assembling the Quilt Top

1. Arrange the blocks into three rows of three blocks each, following the puzzle solution. Sew a yellow 1½" x 18½" strip between each of the large blocks in each row. Press.

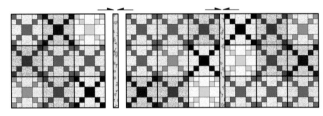

Make 3.

2. Sew three yellow 1½" x 18½" strips with two assorted dark dot 1½" squares. Press. Make two horizontal sashing strips.

Make 2.

3. Sew a sashing strip from step 2 between each of the block rows; then sew the rows together.

4. Sew three yellow 1½" x 18½" rectangles with two assorted dark dot 1½" squares. Press. Make four inner-border strips. Sew an assorted dark dot 1½" square to each end of two of the inner borders. Press.

Make 4 inner borders.

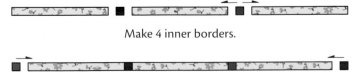

Make 2.

5. Sew three light purple print 1½" x 16½" strips with six assorted dark dot 1½" squares and four light purple print 1½" squares as shown. Press. Make four middle borders. Sew one assorted dark dot 1½" square to both ends of two of the middle borders. Press.

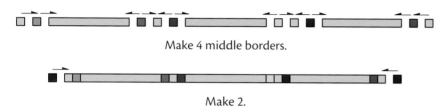

Make 4 middle borders.

Make 2.

6. Sew the shorter inner borders from step 4 to opposite sides of the quilt. Press. Sew the longer inner borders to the top and bottom of the quilt. Press. Sew the middle borders from step 5 to the quilt top in the same manner.

7. Sew the purple-and-yellow print 6½" x 60½" strips to opposite sides of the quilt. Press. Sew the purple-and-yellow print 6½" x 72½" strips to the top and bottom of the quilt. Press.

Finishing the Quilt

1. Layer your quilt with batting and a pieced backing; baste. Quilt as desired. The quilt shown was quilted with curved lines to balance the geometric design.

2. Trim the edges of the quilt layers even with the quilt top and use the purple 2½" x 42" strips to bind the quilt.

About the Author

CYNDI HERSHEY became interested in quilting in 1976 as a result of reading the *Good Housekeeping* issue that featured the Great American Quilt Festival. Since there were very few quilt shops at that time, she taught herself to quilt (with varying results!). Her education and background in interior design and textiles have been helpful as her interest in quilting has grown over the years.

Cyndi began teaching in the early 1980s at shops as well as at community evening schools. In 1989, Cyndi and her husband, Jim, bought the Country Quilt Shop (now Country Quiltworks) located in Montgomeryville, Pennsylvania. Their shop was selected as one of the top 10 quilt shops by *American Patchwork & Quilting* magazine in 1999. They owned the shop for 11 years.

Cyndi currently works for P&B Textiles as a product manager as well as for Martingale & Company as a technical editor. She still considers teaching to be her favorite part of quilting and welcomes inquiries regarding teaching classes. (See the link for teacher resources on Martingale & Company's Web site at www.martingale-pub.com.) Cyndi and her husband live in the Philadelphia suburb of Audubon, Pennsylvania; their family includes four grown children and two grandchildren.